Ride the Giant Waves with Garrett McNamara

Carol Parenzan Smalley

Authorized Biography

Mitchell Lane
PUBLISHERS

P.O. Box 196
Hockessin, Delaware 19707
Visit us on the web: www.mitchelllane.com
Comments? email us: mitchelllane@mitchelllane.com

Mitchell Lane PUBLISHERS

Printing   1   2   3   4   5   6   7   8   9

Extreme Sports
Extreme Cycling with Dale Homes
Extreme Skateboarding with Paul Rodriguez
Ride the Giant Waves with Garrett McNamara
Ultra Running with Scott Jurek

Library of Congress Cataloging-in-Publication Data
Smalley, Carol Parenzan, 1960–
    Ride the giant waves with Garrett McNamara / by Carol Parenzan Smalley.
        p. cm. — (A Robbie reader. Extreme sports)
    Includes bibliographical references and index.
    ISBN 1-58415-486-1 (lib. bdg: alk. paper)
    1. McNamara, Garrett, 1967 — Juvenile literature. 2. Surfers — United States —
Biography — Juvenile literature. I. Title. II. Series.
        GV838.M36S63 2006
        797.3'20 92 — dc22
                                                                    2005036703
ISBN-10: 1-58415-486-1   ISBN-13: 9781584154860

ABOUT THE AUTHOR: Carol Parenzan Smalley loves water. As a child, she swam competitively, and her best stroke was butterfly. She studied water at The Pennsylvania State University, where she earned a degree in environmental engineering. Today, she and her family live in a log cabin in the Adirondack Mountains of upstate New York. She is a master's level competitive swimmer and spends hours by the lakes and rivers in the mountains. She is the author of several other books for young readers, including two biographies (*DaMarcus Beasley* and *Henry Hudson*) for Mitchell Lane Publishers. In addition to homeschooling her daughter and conducting author workshops, she is an online college instructor, where she teaches writing and small business skills.

PHOTO CREDITS: Cover, pp. 1, 3, 4 — Bruno Lemos; p. 6 — Andrea Pickens; pp. 8, 9 — Malia McNamara; p. 12 — Ramon Dapena; p. 14 — Yannic; p. 16 (top) — Bruno Lemos; pp. 16 (bottom), 19 — Sean Davey; p. 21 — Ramon Dapena; p. 22 — Sean Davey; p. 24 — Greg Huglin; p. 25 — Tim McKenna; p. 26 — Connie McNamara

PUBLISHER'S NOTE: This book has been authorized and approved for print by Garrett McNamara. It is based on personal interviews with Garrett McNamara conducted by author Carol Parenzan Smalley in August through October 2005 and by editor Susan Wilkins in February 2006. While every possible effort has been made to ensure accuracy, the publisher will not assume liability for damages caused by inaccuracies in the data.

DISCLAIMER: The sport of surfing should not be attempted without extensive training, experience, proper protective gear, and professional assistance. This is both a high risk and dangerous sport and may result in or cause serious injury to oneself or another and may even cause death. Always consult with a trained professional in surfing before trying this sport. Mitchell Lane Publishers shall not be held liable for any injuries to or damages caused by individuals attempting this sport. *Always Put Safety First.*

TABLE OF CONTENTS

*Words in **bold type** can be found in the glossary.

World-champion tow-in surfer Garrett pries open the mouth of Jaws in Maui, Hawaii, on December 16, 2005. Jaws is one of Garrett's favorite training locations.

JAWS

Like a big shark, the wave tried to eat Garrett McNamara (GAIR-it MAK-na-mayr-uh). It stretched its mouth 50 feet toward the blue Hawaiian (huh-WY-in) sky. White froth poured from its mouth like saliva.

Balanced on his surfboard, Garrett tucked under the wave's lip. The wave, called Jaws, licked Garrett's shoulders and face, blinding him. Once. Twice. Three times. His heart pumped wildly inside his chest. He felt the pull on his feet inside the **footstraps** holding him to his board. He could hear nothing but silence.

And then with the energy of a winter **avalanche** (AA-vuh-lanch), the wave exploded. It vomited Garrett from its mouth. Garrett felt as if he had been picked up by a powerful tornado and tossed across the Pacific Ocean.

He opened his eyes. He was not hurt. It was a ride he would never forget. For 38-year-old Garrett McNamara, it was his best day in the history of extreme surfing.

In extreme surfing, surfers are towed out into the ocean behind **skidoos** (skee-DOOZ) to ride monster-sized waves. The surfers are propelled onto and into the wave using the machine's power. It is a dangerous team sport. It combines fear with fun.

Surfers come from all over the world to tame the wave known as Jaws. But on November 26, 2003, no one controlled it better than Garrett McNamara. On this day, Garrett McNamara, or G-Mac, showed the world why he is the current **tow-in** or extreme surfing champion of the world.

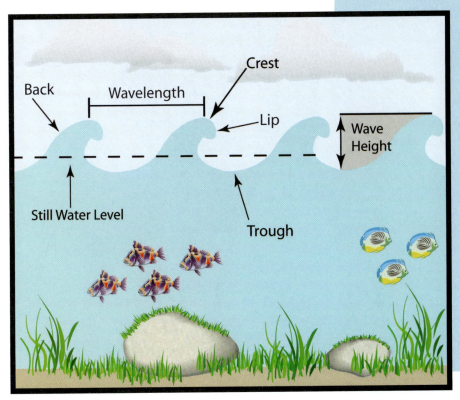

A wave's height is measured from its trough, the lowest point, to its crest, the highest point. Garrett dreams of being the first extreme surfer to ride a wave that is 100 feet high or greater.

Each wave has parts. The *crest* is the highest part. The *trough* (trawf) is the lowest. The *lip* is the part at the top that curls under. *Wave height* is measured from trough to crest. The distance between waves is the *wavelength*. It is measured from crest to crest. The *wave face* points toward the beach, and its *back* points away.

Fourteen-year-old Garrett poses with his favorite extreme sports equipment – the surfboard. Two years earlier, in 1978, a friend introduced him to surfing when Garrett's family moved to Hawaii.

DESTINATION: HAWAII

Young Garrett McNamara surfed the television channels in his family home in Berkeley (BIRK-lee), California. He found *ABC's Wide World of Sports.* On this program, he watched surfers compete on big waves along the coast of Hawaii. He never dreamed that he would one day live in Hawaii or that he would be a world-champion surfer.

In 1978, twelve-year-old Garrett, his younger brother, Liam (LEE-uhm), and his mother, Malia (mah-LEE-uh), moved to Hawaii. They were *malihini* (MAH-lee-hee-nee), or newcomers, to Waialua (wy-uh-LOO-ah) on the Hawaiian island of **Oahu** (oh-WAH-hoo). His father, Laurence (LAW-rins), did not go with them.

The two boys were students at Waialua Elementary School. Their mother encouraged them to do well in school. She also wanted them to be carefree *keiki* (KAY-kee), or children, too.

On a Hawaiian beach at Waimea (wy-MAY-ah) Bay, Garrett and Liam pretended to be racecar drivers. They let the waves hit their

In Pupukea, Hawaii, 17-year-old Garrett McNamara prepares to surf. He had conquered his first ten-foot-high wave one year earlier.

backs. Then they would hit their imaginary gas pedals and race up the beach.

Their mother encouraged Garrett and his brother to learn how to surf. They thought surfing was like skateboarding, but instead of wiping out on hard asphalt (AS-fawlt) or concrete, they'd land on soft water.

Garrett's *brada* (BRAA-duh), or friend, lent him a kneeboard to try. It was about four feet long and two feet wide. Garrett didn't want to ride the waves on his knees. He wanted to stand up. He wanted to be a real surfer.

Garrett surfed as often as he could. He studied rides of famous surfers, like Kerry Terikena, Marvin Foster, and Brock Little. Garrett rode his first 10-foot wave when he was 16.

Garrett worked hard in school, too. He graduated from Waialua High School in 1985. He learned math skills that he uses today to build better surfboards and to size up the monster waves he loves to ride.

G-Mac builds his endurance and fine-tunes his balance on a trampoline in his Wiamea (Hawaii) backyard. Extreme sports athletes, including tow-in surfers, require extreme training.

EXTREME TRAINING

Garrett McNamara knows that it takes hard work to be the best. He is showing the surfing world that age does not matter. Garrett earned his first world title at the age of 35. Today, he is still the world champion.

Garrett wakes early each day. He checks his computer for messages from businesspeople. He e-mails other surfers around the world. He looks at web sites connected to video cameras to check wave conditions (kun-DIH-shuns). Waves can be gnarly (NAR-lee), or extremely rough and dangerous. They can be awesome, or perfect. They can be **hollow,** with big, round

Garrett rides a gnarly wave in Tahiti in 2003. Extreme surfers keep careful watch on wave conditions around the world using web cams. They are ready to travel at a moment's notice to their next extreme adventure.

barrels to ride inside. Or they can be mushy, or weak.

Then it's time to train. First, Garrett rides his bike as fast as he can up Pupukea (pu-pu-KAY-uh) Hill behind his house. This strengthens his legs and helps build his lungs.

He lifts weights at the gym. He also does push-ups and sit-ups. Sometimes Garrett holds his breath when he exercises. He practices using energy with little oxygen (OK-sih-jun). He pretends that he is under the water, where he must not panic.

If the waves are good, Garrett grabs his board and heads to the beach. His favorite place to extreme surf is Jaws on the island of **Maui.** Sometimes he does **traditional surfing**—without a skidoo—at Sunset Beach on Oahu. His brother Liam is a champion traditional surfer. Sometimes they practice together.

If the waves are not good, G-Mac does other water exercises. Sometimes he dives down into underwater caves and swims for two minutes while holding his breath. Other times, he dives down about 40 feet and picks up a 100-pound rock. He runs for one minute on the ocean floor. Garrett can hold his breath for more than three minutes! For safety, he often trains with his teammate Kealii Mamala (kah-AH-lee-ee mah-MAH-luh).

Tow-in teammates Kealii Mamala (left) and Garrett enjoy watching competitors tackle a giant wave in Teahupoo (CHOH-poo), Tahiti. Tow-in surfing requires teamwork and trust in each other.

Mamala (left) and Garrett model extreme-surfing apparel in Haleiwa (hah-lay-EE-vah), Hawaii. Extreme surfing requires special safety equipment, including helmets and life jackets (under shirt).

IT TAKES TWO TO TOW

It takes two strong athletes to make a solid tow-in surfing team. Since 2005, Garrett's partner has been Kealii Mamala. Garrett says Kealii is "just as focused on riding the big waves as I am."

Some waves are too powerful to paddle into. In the past, surfers became frustrated. They wanted to ride the giant waves, but they could not reach them. Garrett remembers drawing cartoon surfers riding huge waves. Back then, riding these giant waves was only a dream.

In 1992, three surfers—Derrick Doerner, Buzzy Kerbox, and Laird Hamilton—dreamed up tow-in surfing . Giant-wave surfing became a reality. The three surfers used an inflatable Zodiac (ZOH-dee-ak) raft with an outboard motor to reach waves breaking far from shore over outer reefs. But the inflatable boats weren't speedy or safe enough. The surfers could not move as fast as the waves they were trying to catch.

The three quickly realized that skidoos could travel as fast as the waves. With a skidoo, they could catch and ride any wave.

In tow-in surfing, one team member drives the skidoo. He pulls the other surfer on his surfboard onto the wave using a very long **towline.** Once he releases the surfer, the driver is responsible

While a rescue team watches, G-Mac shows the form that won him the North Shore Tow-in Championship in Hawaii in January 2006. Garrett has been winning extreme-surfing world championship cups since 2002.

for the surfer's safety. He must know where the surfer is at all times and be prepared to rescue him.

Garrett McNamara began tow-in surfing in 1994. He switched from a traditional surfboard to one that was shorter, narrower, thinner, heavier, and much faster. Sometimes he adds extra weights to his surfboard. The weights allow him to stay on the water and keep up the momentum (moh-MEN-tum), or speed moving forward.

Garrett and Kealii share more than waves. They also share sponsors (SPON-surs). Sponsors are companies that help the team by providing money and equipment. It is expensive to travel around the world and surf big waves.

Garrett poses with numerous surfboards. He uses the math skills he learned in school to design his specialized surfing equipment.

Garrett brought a new height to tow-in surfing on January 30, 2006, when he was placed by helicopter onto the face of a giant wave in Haleiwa, Hawaii. The waves are too large and dangerous to paddle into, so competitors are released onto the waves.

HOW EXTREME WILL GARRETT GO?

For Garrett McNamara, there are no limits for extreme surfing. In January 2006, he was even towed in by a helicopter!

Garrett hopes to one day see extreme surfing as an Olympic (oh-LIM-pik) sport. Surfers are still waiting to ride the first 100-foot wave. For Garrett, the wave will have to be greater than 100 feet, so there will be no doubt that it truly counts.

In 2006, G-Mac worked with a television producer to create an extreme surfing program and reality show. He is in an **IMAX** (EYE-maks) film about the sport called *Big Wave Hunters*. Garrett also surfs in the 2006 DVD *Shark Park: The Heaviest Wave in California.* The movie is about a remote offshore reef during the 2005–2006 giant winter swells. He travels around the world riding the biggest and best waves.

Garrett kicks away from his surfboard while filming *Shark Park: The Heaviest Wave in California* during the winter of 2005–2006. He also starred in an IMAX film called *Big Wave Hunters*.

After wiping out in a big barrel and slamming the reef in Teahupoo, Tahiti, Garrett sports an injured leg. Surfing buddy Koby Alberton rides the skidoo with him. Injuries are common in extreme sports. Garrett has needed more than 500 stitches in his surfing career.

In his surfing career, G-Mac has broken his back, ribs, feet, and one hand. He has needed at least 500 stitches. He is not afraid of the giant waves or of getting injured. But he does respect the ocean and its monster waves. He knows that every wave, like every person, has its own personality (pur-suh-NAL-uh-tee).

25

Six-year-old daughter Ariana (center, born 1995) poses with her cousins Makai (left) and Ladon McNamara. Garrett's family comes first in his life, followed closely by his faith in God and giant waves.

Six-year-old Titus (born 1997) shares his passion for surfing with his father. Garrett McNamara encourages young athletes to dream big and work hard to achieve those dreams.

Garrett's family is the center point of his life. Along with his faith in God, he is supported by his wife, Connie, and cheered on by their two children. His daughter, Ariana (ayr-ee-AH-nuh), was born in 1995. She likes to play soccer. His son, Titus (TY-tus), was born in 1997. He dreams of being a champion extreme surfer like his dad.

Garrett encourages young surfers interested in extreme surfing to work hard at the sport and on their ability to focus. "There's no room to mess around in the big waves," says Garrett. "Do everything you can do to become physically (FIH-zuh-klee), mentally, and spiritually prepared. Put your mind to it." Garrett suggests that young surfers determine their goals and train hard. "If you put your heart and soul into something and do the necessary steps, you can do it. Dreams do come true."

Garrett dreams of guiding younger surfers into the sport. And he dreams of riding the biggest monster wave ever. **Aloha** (uh-LOH-ha).

CHRONOLOGY

1967 Born on August 10 in Pittsfield, Massachusetts

1969 Family moves to Berkeley, California

1978 Moves with mother, Malia, and brother, Liam, to Hawaii; surfs for the first time

1983 Rides first 10-foot wave

1985 Graduates from Waialua High School

1992 Extreme or tow-in surfing is pioneered

1994 Switches from traditional surfing to tow-in surfing

1995 Marries Connie; daughter, Ariana, is born

1997 Son, Titus, is born

2002 Wins first extreme surfing world championship with partner Rodrigo "Monster" Rosenda

2003 Wins second extreme surfing world championship with partner Ikaika Kalama; rides Jaws, the best barrel wave ever ridden

2005 Holds title of reigning world cup extreme surfer; films IMAX movie *Big Wave Hunters*; begins work on extreme surfing television show; partners up with Kealii Mamala

2006 Experiences helicopter tow-in in January; with Mamala, wins North Shore Tow-In Championships in Hawaii; appears in the DVD *Shark Park: The Heaviest Wave in California*

GLOSSARY

aloha (uh-LOH-ha)—The Hawaiian word for hello and goodbye.

avalanche (AA-vuh-lanch)—A large amount of snow moving down a mountain.

barrel (BAA-rul)—A wave that forms a tunnel.

footstraps Devices that attach a surfer's feet to a surfboard.

hollow Surfer slang for a wave with a barrel or tunnel.

IMAX (EYE-maks)—A movie format where the screen is several stories high and moviegoers sit in stadium-like setting.

Maui (MOW-ee)—One of the Hawaiian Islands.

Oahu (ah-WAH-hoo)—The main island of Hawaii.

skidoo (skee-DOO)—A small, motorized watercraft used in extreme surfing.

tow-in surfing A type of surfing where the surfer is towed by a skidoo onto a gaint wave and released.

towline The rope used to tow a surfer behind a skidoo.

traditional surfing (trah-DIH-shah-nul)—Surfing waves at the shoreline without the help of a skidoo.

FIND OUT MORE

Books

Berger, Melvin and Gilda. *What Makes an Ocean Wave?: Questions and Answers About Oceans and Ocean Life.* New York: Scholastic Inc., 2000.

Chapman, Garry. *Extreme Sports: Surf.* Broomall, Pennsylvania: Chelsea House Publishers, 2001.

Mauer, Tracy Nelson. *Radsports Guides: Surfing. Vero Beach, Florida:* Rourke Publishing LLC, 2003.

Souza, D. M. *Powerful Waves.* Minneapolis: Carolrhoda Books, Inc., 1992.

Voeller, Edward. *Extreme Surfing.* Mankato, Minnesota: Capstone Books, 2000.

Works Consulted

This biography is based on personal interviews with Garrett McNamara by Carol Parenzan Smalley, August–October 2005, and by Susan Wilkins, February 23, 2006.

Global Surf News, "Interview with Garrett McNamara and Big Wednesday Story." http://www.globalsurfnews.com/news.asp?Id_news=15614

McNamara, Garrett. "Garrett's Bio: Garrett 'G-Mac' McNamara." http://www.garrettmcnamara.com/biography.htm

Moringa, Dayton. "McNamara, Mamala Tow In a Big Victory." *Honolulu Advertiser,* posted February 10, 2006, http://the.honoluluadvertiser.com/article/2006/Feb/10/sp/FP602100355.html

Neptune's Web. "Waves and Tides: The Anatomy of a Wave."
http://pao.cnmoc.navy.mil/educate/neptune/quest/wavetide/
anatomy.htm

Novak, Flynn. "Garrett McNamera [sic] and Ikaika Kalama," *Next Action
Sports,* July–August 2005.

On the Internet

Readers are invited to contact Garrett McNamara to learn more about
surfing through his official web site
htpp://www.garrettmcnamara.com

Kealii Mamala's offical website
http://www.kealiimamala.com

Association of Professional Tow Surfers
http://www.protowsurfers.org

National Scholastic Surfing Association

http://www.nssa.org

Nuit de la Glisse, "Riders: Garrett McNamara"
http://www.nuitdelaglisse.com

Surfer Magazine

http://www.surfermag.com

Surfing Magazine

http://www.surfingthemag.com

Tow Surfer

http://www.towsurfer.com

INDEX